Robert Alves and Don Robertson
Contributing Editor: Marty Rabenovets

Edition

THE ASSOCIATION EXEC's

GUIDE TO IMPROVING ORGANIZATIONAL PERFORMANCE

HOW TO MAKE SURE YOUR BUSINESS STRATEGY DRIVES YOUR TECHNOLOGY INVESTMENTS

Printed in the United States of America

Second Edition, 2016

First published, 2015

ISBN: 978-1-329-13930-5

Advanced Solutions International (ASI)
901 N. Pitt Street, Suite 200
Alexandria, VA 22314
www.advsol.com

TABLE OF CONTENTS

From the Authors

As you know massive change has occurred in the way associations like yours communicate with members. Here's an example of how fast this change is occurring: Just look at the photos below showing the difference between the groups of people who showed up at the Vatican in 2005 to welcome Pope Benedict compared to those who welcomed Pope Francis in 2013.[1] Nearly everyone in the crowd in the newer photo is using a mobile device.

More than likely, the systems you bought just a few years ago — and still use today to manage your member data — were not designed and conceived to take full advantage of the Internet. And, they are probably now just about obsolete because they cannot adequately handle your needs in a changing and fast-moving world.

If you are considering making technology investments anytime in the next three years, Advanced Solutions International (ASI) can help you now. The two of us co-founded ASI in 1991 and have grown it to the largest, founder-owned software company in the world for member and donor-based not-for-profits.

---

[1] 2005 photo: AP Photo/Luca Bruno; 2013 photo: AP Photo/Michael Sohn.

We wrote this book specifically with C-level leaders in mind. So, please don't delegate looking at it to your department managers. This conversation is simply too important and too high-level. It centers on topics your department managers are not comfortable discussing and ones that, frankly, need your leadership to make the tough decisions that will successfully navigate your organization into the future. You'll want to be sure to take full advantage of what we have to offer. This book is based on our work since 1991 with more than 2,500 associations and 1,500 other not-for-profit clients in more than 25 countries.

We believe we have found important answers to the questions you should be asking about how to position your association for the future. We have found our most successful clients make sure their business strategy drives their technology investments. These clients learn about themselves continuously from their operational activities. As a result, they use this knowledge to continuously improve their organization's performance.

To help clients move forward as quickly and confidently as possible, ASI created a special program called the "Success Partnership Program" (SPP) that identifies your most pressing problems, helps you get organized, saves you time and money, lowers your risk of investing in the wrong technology assets, and keeps you from being disappointed once again because you did not achieve the expected return on your investment. This *"Performance Improvement Preview"* is just one of the valuable resources we offer and we'll discuss in the following pages.

The leaders of our client organizations see us as a trusted advisor for their strategic investments in technology.

We offer a unique approach to help you align your strategy and operations so that your future investments result in long-term, continuous performance improvement — instead of needing to start over every five to seven years. More than 750 clients have been with us for 15 years or more; they're accruing major benefits from their technology investments because they are getting great results year after year.

In the following pages we don't just talk theory. We provide the hands-on tools you need — proven best practice strategies, solutions to problems, self-assessments, and results-based case studies from real clients to help you gain insight into what you must do if you want to adapt to the massive changes upon us. Our intention is to "lift the veil" and share behind-the-scenes insights that can show you how to avoid modern-day software selection and implementation pitfalls while aligning your strategy and technology to create a lasting advantage for your organization. Most importantly, we show you how to achieve continuous performance improvement for your organization.

We offer you this book as a practical resource. Use it wisely and the rewards will be great!

Wishing you great success,

Robert Alves
Chairman and CEO

Don Robertson
President and CTO

Advanced Solutions International (ASI)

Chapter 1 — Making Yourself the Leader of Your Technology Investments

Like most association executives today, you're no doubt looking for the best ways to successfully lead your organization into the future. But, how on earth do you do this when technology is changing so quickly, the economy is still sluggish, and your members' needs are constantly growing and becoming more sophisticated?

In his book, *Race for Relevance*, Harrison Coerver talks about the need for leaders of not- for-profits to approach technology investments in a new and different way. He goes on to say:

> "***The adoption and exploitation of technology, particularly information and communication technologies, must become an integral component of the organization's functioning and performance.***"[2]

But to make this happen, senior leadership needs to be directly engaged. Mr. Coerver makes these and other great points that we will continue to drive home throughout our book.

---

[2] Harrison Coerver and Mary Byers, Race for Relevance (Washington, DC: ASAE) Kindle edition.

In working with more than 4,000 clients since 1991, Advanced Solutions International (ASI), has become the largest, founder-owned software company in the world for associations and not-for-profits. Through this work, we've earned our position as a trusted advisor to the executives of these organizations and have learned the most successful best-practice lessons first-hand.

We're going to share the behind-the-scenes tips and strategies you'll need to:

- Increase membership engagement/retention
- Reduce costs, and
- Improve overall organizational performance

Using Best Practices to Lead Your Team

Over the years, we've learned a lot from our clients and they've learned a lot from us as well. The most successful association CEOs adhere to the following four best practices that stand out from all the rest:

1) **Let the business strategy drive technology decision making**. With a clear business strategy you can design your operational systems and activities to achieve your goals. This is the basis for an environment of continuous performance improvement.
2) **Focus on becoming a "continuous learning organization."** You must learn from your operational activities all the time, at every step of the way, to realize continuous performance improvement.

3) **Ensure your data is accurate, up-to-date and easily accessible.** Clean, real-time data that can be reported on and analyzed is crucial to continuous performance improvement — you can never underestimate its importance.
4) **Recognize that your website is your business system and vice versa**. You can no longer separate the two —a website providing personalized, dynamic content based on your member data, is your future engine for engagement and retention.

Top 4 Association Best Practices

1) ***Let your business strategy drive technology decision making.***
2) ***Focus on becoming a "continuous learning organization."***
3) ***Ensure your data is accurate, up-to-date, and easily accessible.***
4) ***Recognize that your website is your business system and vice versa.***

Examining Your Existing Tools to Enable Continuous Performance Improvement

Our vision for success as your trusted advisor is to help you see that an Engagement Management System (EMS) is a critical management tool — not "just software." We want to help you enable continuous performance improvement in your organization by using EMS tools to help you constantly learn from your business activities and ultimately reach your goals. Adopting the Engagement Management System mindset allows our clients to embrace the growing importance of their members as key users of their systems, whether from a mobile device or traditional PC.

> ***What is Continuous Performance Improvement?***
>
> This is a systematic process that can include creating scorecards to measure results, establishing key performance indicators (KPIs), accessing real-time data to make informed decisions, and implementing a system that allows adjustments/improvements on the fly — all to Improve the operational performance of the organization.
>
> *[See Chapter 5 for more detail.]*

We also want to help you understand the importance of learning from these transactions. To do this successfully, all member activities need to be collected in a single database and all data needs to be easily accessible for analysis. Your EMS must work the way the world works today so you can capture this data in real time.

We all know the last few years have brought massive change to the communication and information technologies we use. Consequently, your members are changing how they communicate with you — and faster than you think. Therefore, your member management system needs to be able to adapt to and support these changes. Private communities, social engagement, on-line commerce, on-line dues payments, etc. must be part of your Engagement Management System.
This means you need to embrace the idea that your business system is your website and vice versa.

To adapt to the massive changes happening you must be willing to fuse your database and your website into one easy-to-use application. Your website needs to allow members convenient self-service options so that they can do whatever they need and want to do from anywhere they want, at any time they want, and from any device they choose.

Your website needs to allow members convenient self-service options so that they can do whatever they need and want to do from anywhere they want, at any time they want, and from any device they choose.

At the end of 2014, more on-line commercial orders were placed in the USA with mobile devices than with PCs.

This means you need to be ready. It's vital that your business system/website offers the flexibility you'll need to make necessary changes on-the-fly to ensure members have the options they need to make their lives easier and keep them engaged with your organization.

When we work with new clients, many are surprised that we talk about helping them make the best decisions all the way through the selection/implementation process. We do this to ensure they're able to improve their organizational performance.

This book provides a blueprint to help you achieve the following:

1) Choose a member management system that can effectively support your organization as technology continues to change.
2) Increase your member engagement/retention and, as a result, continuously improve your performance. This results in excess resources you can reinvest in your association year after year.
3) Conduct a *"Performance Improvement Preview"* of a modern system before you make a technology investment.

We don't have sales executives, we have "Performance Improvement Specialists" who bring that unique perspective and focus to every meeting they have with clients.

Practical Options for Leading Your Team to Smart Technology Investments

Another unique advantage ASI offers is our "Success Partnership Program." This includes a *"Performance Improvement Preview"* that lets potential clients see our iMIS 20 Engagement Management System (EMS) in a real-world environment using their own data and processes. We make this innovative program available to association executives like you because we're confident that it will show you precisely how you can benefit from our expertise as trusted advisors to thousands of organizations worldwide.

> ***The Success Partnership Program (SPP) includes a "Performance Improvement Preview" that lets potential clients experience our iMIS 20 Engagement Management System.***

Many of your peers have already taken advantage of this program and you should, too. There's no risk — you come away with a personalized requirements document you can use to make a highly informed decision about your future technology investments no matter what you decide to invest in or who you work with.

How to Use this Book

We cite a lot of data in this book. Our primary research is internal — based on our experience with 4,000 associations and other not-for-profits worldwide. We gather many success stories and best practices from the field — working with clients like you. We have also conducted a global survey of membership executives and published it in our 2016 Global Benchmark Report on Membership Performance (see the addendum for an executive summary of the report.)

Our secondary research comes from formal studies, such as the annual Lehman Associates' Association Software Global Study, studies from the TCC research group, and other sources, all of which focus on the not-for-profit space.

This book is divided into three major sections:

- An outline of the challenges that associations are currently facing — some of which you may recognize and a few that you perhaps weren't even aware of.
- An overview of the new Engagement Management System (EMS) that can tackle the challenges of today and tomorrow.
- A summary of the results you can expect to achieve with an EMS.

We've also included lots of tips, self-assessment exercises and success stories you can learn from. We invite you to take full advantage of the advice we've gathered to propel your association forward.

Chapter 2 — Assessing Your Current Situation

Before you dive into the tips, strategies, and best practices we've loaded into this book, it's important to stop and take stock of your organization.

> ***... the behavior that distinguishes quality association leadership is execution of tactics and tasks that propel the association towards achieving its stated mission and strategy.***

Often times, when working with senior executives, strategy has an independent life of its own. Senior management teams love to strategize and boldly proclaim their mission and member-service commitments on their websites. The public communication of strategy appeals to those who want to separate themselves from the day-to-day tedium of managing a successful association. But the behavior that separates the quality association management teams from the rest is execution of tactics and tasks that propel the association forward making progress towards its stated mission and strategy. In our experience this is harder to find than one might think. Strategy is important but strategy without execution is worthless.

The world is full of great ideas and even internally and externally sponsored studies on what you should do to increase the impact of your association. But, prior to exploring the successful action steps you should implement, we ask that you take the 25-point Success Assessment below. This will help set a benchmark for where your organization is today compared to where it should be.

25-Point Success Assessment

This Association Success Assessment breaks down the four areas that contribute to not-for-profit success—***Recruit, Engage, Measure, and Grow***.

Each individual section is strategically important to your business success and links to a collective approach that will help you reach your mission objectives and profitability goals. Indicators of success in one section but failure in another will help you and your team identify operational gaps hindering maximum organizational performance.

By evaluating your group's ability to implement and sustain an integrated revenue capture program, our process can help you take steps not just to survive but to thrive. All information collected is confidential.

The questions probe strategic and tactical issues on how your organization operates.

Is this the end analysis of your organization's ability to grow revenue? No, of course not, but the Association Success Assessment does help you identify specific gaps in your organization's best practices approach and peak performance capabilities.

Check the box that most accurately applies to your membership organization. If the question does not apply, skip it. If you can't answer the question but it does apply to your current business model, seek the appropriate department head and ask for an answer. If you can't get a clear answer, select "No."

Recruit:

How do you recruit new members and retain existing ones with integrated, multi-channel marketing campaigns.

1. Do you have a written and automated strategic plan to recruit members in underserved groups within your prospect base?

   ☐ Yes ☐ No

2. Do you and your executive team regularly review reports that track the number of member service calls that are not completed (or not responded to) in the same day and then carried over to the next day?

   ☐ Yes ☐ No

3. Do you have a written and automated process designed to welcome, thank and retain new members effectively so they feel that becoming involved with your group is a good use of their time and money?

   ☐ Yes ☐ No

4. Does your information system provide reports or other ways to analyze what your new and current members expect from your organization so that you can effectively tailor marketing and service messages in your communications?

   ☐ Yes ☐ No

5. Does your membership recruitment team have sufficient time each week to identify and speak with prospective members personally?

   ☐ Yes ☐ No

Engage:

Empower members to engage with your organization and with other members – anytime, anywhere.

6. Do you have a consistent written and automated process for sustaining member engagement at a high level so that you have a large pool of future volunteer leaders?

   ☐ Yes ☐ No

7. Do you have a written and implemented method for simplifying, standardizing and automating business processes to manage the business operations you execute annually more efficiently?

   ☐ Yes ☐ No

8. Can you monitor whether each staff member is following the agreed-upon business rules and practices for using information systems set by your leadership team so that you can rely on the data in the system when making strategic decisions?

☐ Yes ☐ No

9. Do you have a written and implemented process to train new employees on fundamental processes and tasks within your organization so they can become immediately productive?

☐ Yes ☐ No

10. Are at least 90% of member email addresses, mailing addresses, and phone numbers on file confirmed, current and accurate so that you can communicate effectively with each of your member groups instantly?

☐ Yes ☐ No

11. Do you have written and automated procedures in place that are implemented by your staff to satisfactorily address member support issues?

☐ Yes ☐ No

12. Do you regularly measure how happy and satisfied your members are with your websites, services you offer, and the overall operations of your organization, so you can share this information with staff to tailor future services and develop new programs?

☐ Yes ☐ No

Measure:

Continually measure and improve marketing campaigns and member engagement efforts.

13. Does your organization use a 12-week over/under cash flow analysis to calculate cash gaps in your operational needs?

☐ Yes ☐ No

14. Can you measure what each member means to your organization in financial terms?

☐ Yes ☐ No

15. Do you calculate projected cash flow operational needs 3 to 5 years out?

☐ Yes ☐ No

16. Do your accounting practices facilitate changing business processes in other departments of your organization and are you able to integrate your accounting system with other information systems, such as member management, event registration, order processing, and online commerce systems— without customization?

☐ Yes ☐ No

17. Can your executive leadership and staff easily access the information you collect about a member at will, without help, from one source (with no information maintained in extraneous / redundant data sources such as Excel spreadsheets, rolodexes and the like) to obtain a complete picture of each member's engagement during his or her involvement with the organization?

☐ Yes ☐ No

18. Do you have current, real-time information proactively available to help you manage strategic, technical, operational and financial needs as they develop?

☐ Yes ☐ No

Grow:

Increase new member acquisition, improve member retention, and identify new revenue opportunities.

19. Various barriers such as organizational silos, inadequate staff training, custom programming, and inadequate financial reserves can inhibit your ability to respond quickly to challenges and opportunities. Are you able to roll out emergency initiatives within a week and major new programs within 60 days?

    ☐ Yes ☐ No

20. Maintaining multiple, diverse revenue sources often requires separate business structures and processes for each. Do you have an effective structure, business processes and trained staff to attract, develop and maintain new sources of revenue?

    ☐ Yes ☐ No

21. Over the last five years, have you averaged consistent membership retention of 90% or more?

    ☐ Yes ☐ No

22. Over the last five years, have you averaged consistent growth of at least 10% per year in members and revenue?

    ☐ Yes ☐ No

23. Does your organization have a written, long-range strategic plan approved by the Board and currently implemented?

☐ Yes ☐ No

24. Does your annual budget provide a written blueprint, reviewed quarterly, that directs your staff on action steps they need to take to achieve your organizational goals for that year and beyond?

☐ Yes ☐ No

25. Are you 100% confident that if either your physical offices became uninhabitable or you lost your key technical staff, neither would cause any downtime for your website and member systems?

☐ Yes ☐ No

Results:

Give yourself 4% for each "yes" answer. The test is not a complete assessment of your revenue growth and performance improvement potential, but a snapshot of where you may be versus where you need to be.

60% and Below

Creating efficiencies that enable your organization to effectively grow each year (even in down markets) will be difficult since your current business success model cannot achieve year-over-year sustainable growth. If your revenues happen to be increasing, this is an anomaly, not a methodology or a business process. It has specific financial and operational leakage issues and corporate instability exposure. To fix this position, you need to redesign your business and the integration of your operations, membership, and strategy processes into one member need-driven approach.

61% to 80%

Your current business growth model has only some of the best practice attributes needed to grow association revenue, year-over-year, using a planned process. Some of your business structure may need to be adjusted to maximize long-term organizational growth goals.

80% and Above

Your association structure maximizes organizational growth capabilities and uses an inter-department alignment that focuses on strategy linked to action steps. You have built a sustainable pattern that should foster continued success for you and your team.

Chapter 3 — The Challenge: Improving Engagement and Organizational Performance

Our internal research — from working with more than 4,000 associations and not-for-profits around the world — shows that the top two problems for membership organizations are: 1) increasing engagement and 2) improving organizational performance.

Engagement involves:

- Member Retention and Acquisition
- Member Satisfaction
- Employee Satisfaction
- Data Integrity
- Brand Enhancement

Improving performance means:

- Reaching Your Goals
- Maximizing Staff Productivity
- Managing Risk
- Controlling Operating Costs
- Keeping up with Changing Technology

Understanding the History of AMS/CRM Systems

Association Management Software (AMS) and Constituent Relationship Management (CRM) software were initially designed for staff that needed to perform administrative tasks, such as processing dues payments and registrations for events. As time went on, organizations decided to add member websites, such as portals and social communities. These supported better engagement of members, but they were all still separate systems, separate projects, and separate budgets. Then, of course, you had to deal with taking financial transactions from these members.

Later, the need arose to connect the association's website with member databases. Most of the time, all of these add-ons to the AMS or CRM system had their own name and address database. And that had to be connected to the main database by programmers doing expensive and time-consuming integration projects.

Today nearly everyone is using mobile devices to get and give information — and your members want to be able to do that through your association's website. This may force the creation of yet another specialized name and address database if you're using a traditional system. All of these databases become silos of information that are not designed to work together. This causes ongoing complexity, which leads to more problems. Supporting different technologies and complex integrations becomes a stumbling block to upgrades.

The total cost of ownership of a traditional AMS/CRM system with these add-ons is skyrocketing. The cost to purchase and maintain products from multiple vendors — as well as the services to support them — is unacceptable. And that doesn't even account for management time. Here's the scary thing: many associations are unaware that they have a choice and don't need to buy this dysfunctional, antiquated model ever again. There is a better, more modern approach that will increase engagement, control costs, and deliver continuous performance improvement.

The diagram below illustrates the many problems of traditional systems.

- ***Complex Integrations***
- ***Disparate Products & Vendors***
- ***Higher Cost of Ownership***

Evaluating Your True Ability to Measure Performance

It might surprise you to know that the traditional systems readily available today are not the best way to meet the challenges of tomorrow. But, no doubt you're already experiencing that first hand. Our findings show that the traditional system that most organizations use today — such as an AMS or CRM system positioned as "state of the art" —cannot deliver continuous performance improvement.

What Does it Cost?

The traditional approach involves multiple systems (to manage member data, websites, mobile, social, etc.) To work together, these systems need to be customized — and this customization needs to be maintained on an ongoing basis by vendors who are essentially incented to keep the system as complicated as possible. This trickles down and causes your staff costs to rise to further support all of the system complexity.

Are Your Management Tools Effective?

Our research shows traditional systems are ineffective management tools. They destroy opportunities for continuous performance improvement because they are often built on disparate databases. This creates roadblocks to any kind of disciplined data management, disconnects operational activities from strategic goals, and leads to unreliable management reporting.

> ***A recent analysis of nearly 2,500 not-for-profits by consulting firm TCC Group has found that those exhibiting multiple 'R&D behaviors," such as gathering data directly from program recipients to determine how to improve programs and evaluating programs to figure out what works, grow revenues more than twice as fast as those not-for-profits exhibiting no such behaviors, even after controlling for other factors.***[3]

But, if your system isn't capable of gathering, analyzing, and then implementing this intelligence, you could be left in the underperforming group.

What Opportunities Are You Losing?

> ***...we estimate that the average association with a traditional system loses a minimum of 10-15% of potential revenue per year due to poor management decisions based on flawed data.***

There is also the problem of high opportunity costs or lost opportunity because traditional systems are ineffective in growing and maintaining member engagement.

---

[3] Peter York, TCC Group Briefing Paper: *Success by Design,* Web, Retrieved January 28, 2015, http://www.tccgrp.com/pdfs/7-21_TCC_Briefing_Paper_LR.pdf

Traditional systems are not suited for the way the world works today — they were built for a time in the past. Associations now need to provide members with convenient, flexible web interfaces that make it easy to engage. They need to provide information exactly how the members want it, when they want it, and from wherever they want it.

There are several reasons the old approach fails, but we estimate that the average association with a traditional system loses a minimum of 10-15% of potential revenue per year due to poor management decisions based on flawed data. Or, in instances when management can't make a decision because they have no data. And that opportunity cost only grows when figuring in lost member engagement and retention.

Since August 2013, a group of organizations (Robert Frances Group, Chaordix Inc., Principal Consulting LLC, and the IBM Information Governance Community) surveyed, interviewed and analyzed data collected from 600 business and IT professionals.[4]

Their results showed that 66% of respondents knew about customer-related problems that stem from poor data quality and 73% acknowledged that poor data caused them to lose some or all of a client's business. While these findings were most prevalent in companies with more than 10,000 employees, they were true for all other size ranges as well. And the lessons of these commercial enterprises are just as relevant for associations.

---

[4] *Enterprise Executive*, "Poor Data Quality Costs More Than You Think," Cal Braunstein and Stuart Selip, November/December 2014, Pages 52-59.

Examining Your Return on Investment (ROI) from Technology

The chart below shows what it might look like over a seven-year period if you invest in a traditional system. Basically, you're going to see weak net revenue gains and weak net revenue contributions. This graph shows that you might grow revenue somewhat from Year 1 to Year 7, but you're also going to see your costs go up. And if revenue and costs go up at the same rate, you're not realizing continuous improvement.

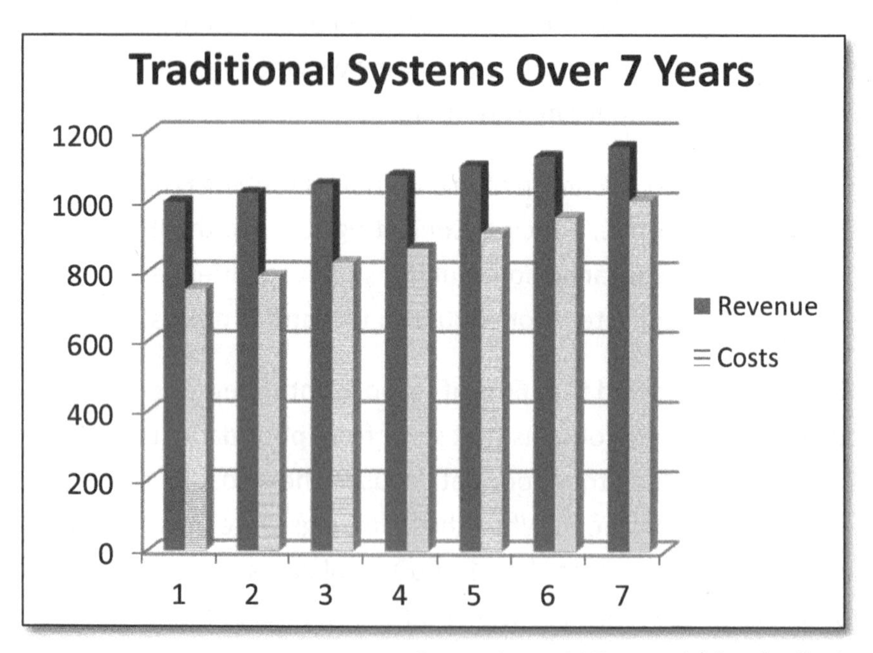

Source: Internal ASI research/client feedback.

Determining What's Driving Up Your Costs

If you select a system today by going to a trade show, hiring a system selection consultant, or relying on conventional wisdom there's a high probability you'll buy a traditional system with disparate solutions cobbled together to meet your needs. This will result in higher costs from multiple applications and vendors, duplication/overlap, and custom services required to support and integrate the various applications to help you address member engagement.

Feedback from our clients about their past experiences shows that services account for more than 60% of AMS and CRM system expenses.

This antiquated traditional model will also greatly increase the amount of internal staff time that goes into managing the old approach. Feedback from our clients about their past experiences shows that services account for more than 60% of AMS and CRM system expenses. The majority of these costs go toward systems integration, customizations, difficult upgrades, and software bug fixes over time.

Assessing Real Costs of Your Technology

You'll see in the chart below that traditional AMS and CRM systems cost a lot more than you think to maximize membership engagement over time. The legend on the right shows all the things you actually need to do to offer the top-class service your members need. So, you may start out with a certain new system budget in Year 1 but by the time you add in all the upgrades, customizations, integrations, etc., those costs could triple by Year 3.

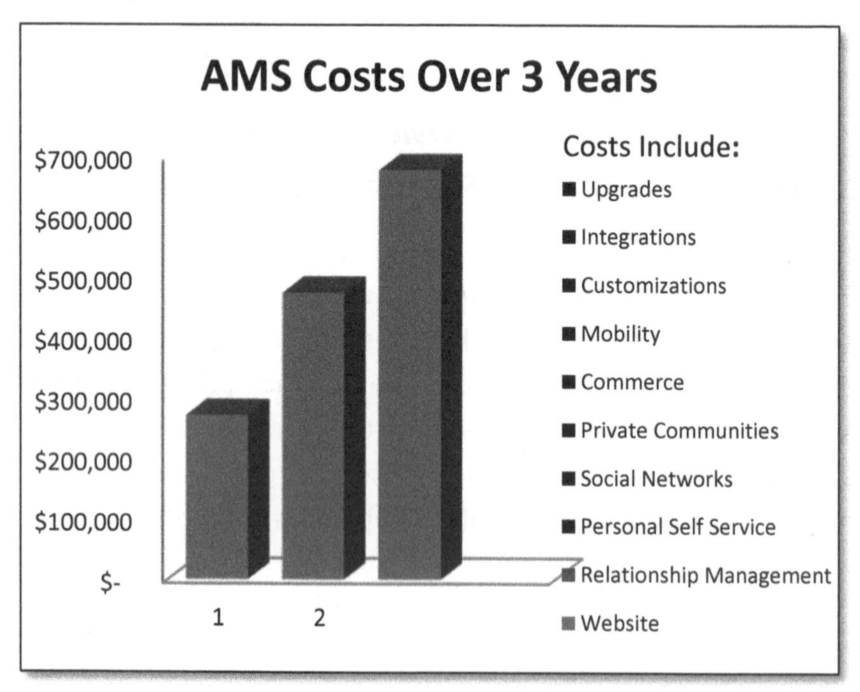

Source: Internal ASI research/client feedback.

Does this surprise you? Well it doesn't end there. There are also hidden costs. Managers and staff have to look after all of these extra elements. They have to manage data silos and they have multiple vendors to deal with. These multiple systems have multiple integration points. That carries overhead. Then there's customization and training. All of this is costly and impacts your management and related staff time.

Assessing Management and Staff Costs of Your Technology

In the three-year timeframe we've discussed, you may see the burden on your staff escalate significantly. You may have to add two staff and deal with the impact on the existing staff to handle the system. So, we're going to add another $360,000 to the first 3 years to account for the staff time in the chart below.

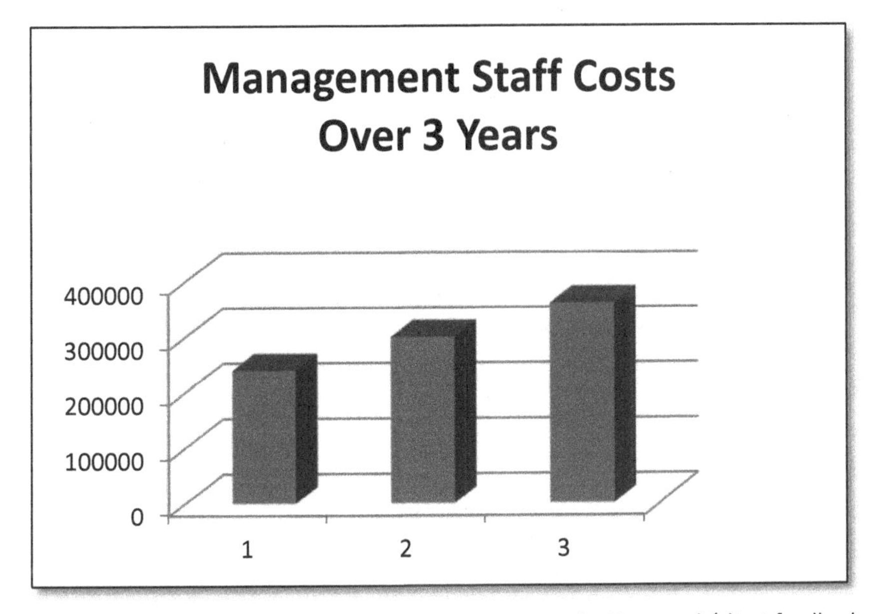

Source: Internal ASI research/client feedback.

Apply Simple Math to All Costs to Get a Real Number

When we add the management impact of these systems into the equation, the costs grow even larger. In this next chart, you can see how a system initially started at $225,000, but the actual cost is $1,037,500 by Year 3 — about 5 times the original cost, when you include the impact on staff. So, no matter what your starting point is, you can expect to spend 400% more with a traditional AMS or CRM system when you factor in the impact of staffing and service costs.

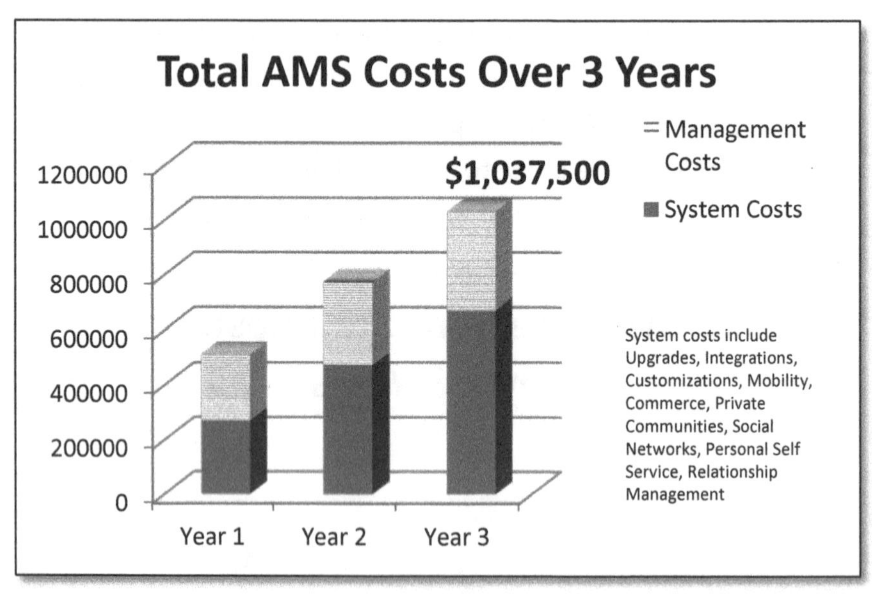

Source: Internal ASI research/client feedback.

Chapter 4 — The Solution: Understanding a Modern Engagement Management System (EMS)

Evaluating Your Management Style

Everyone agrees that massive change is upon us, especially in the areas of information, communications, and the technologies we use for these. Historically, this type of massive change has been a great opportunity for innovation and even re-invention of organizations like yours. However, in 2016 there are powerful vested interests in preserving the status quo. There is a high probability — if you leave technology decisions to your staff or conventional methods — your organization will invest in the wrong technology platform. As with any major change in direction, the mandate must come from the top. The CEO needs to lead the transition.

There is a high probability — if you leave technology decisions to your staff or conventional methods — your organization will invest in the wrong technology platform. As with any major change in direction, the mandate must come from the top. The CEO needs to lead the transition.

[In *Race for* Relevance, one of the most popular not-for-profit management books of the past decade, author Harrison Coerver talks about the need for leaders of not- for-profits to approach technology investments in a new and different way. He goes on to say:

> ***"The adoption and exploitation of technology, particularly information and communication technologies, must become an integral component of the organization's functioning and performance."***[5]

But to make this happen, senior leadership needs to be directly engaged.] Your leadership in making technology decisions could have a pivotal impact on your organization's future success. No one else can bring the strategic perspective into the thinking process.

---

[5] Harrison Coerver and Mary Byers, Race for Relevance (Washington, DC: ASAE) Kindle edition.

You need to let your people know it is okay to think out-of-the-box and let these forward thinking ideas compete with the more traditional ideas. After all, the world has drastically changed.

4 Best Practices That Will Ensure Your Success

In our work with thousands of clients worldwide over the past 20+ years, we've heard a common theme from the most successful organizations — those that have withstood economic pressures, evolving technologies, and demographic changes. They all subscribe to the following four key best practices:

1) **Let the business strategy drive technology decision making**. With a clear business strategy you can design your operational systems and activities to help you achieve your goals. This is the basis for an environment of continuous performance improvement.
2) **Focus on becoming a "continuous learning organization."** You must learn from your operational activities all the time, at every step of the way, to achieve continuous performance improvement.
3) **Ensure your data is accurate, up-to-date and easily accessible.** Clean, real-time data that can be reported on and analyzed is crucial to continuous performance improvement — you can never underestimate its importance.
4) **Recognize that your website is your business system and vice versa**. You can no longer separate the two —a website that provides your members with personalized, dynamic content based on your organization's member data is absolutely critical to engagement and retention.

Our research shows that clients can achieve significant gains from a single, modern system specifically designed for the way associations actually work today.

The greatest gains come from clients who focus on driving continuous performance improvement through best practices. These clients focus on maximizing member engagement, particularly web-based engagement.

To do this, it's a must that you build your new system on a single database and consolidate as many applications as possible to reduce cost and complexity. This includes fusing all member-oriented websites with your member database to create an all-inclusive system. But some things are easy to say and hard to do.

When selecting a new system you want to minimize customization, and invest in a solution that allows you to meet most of your needs right out-of-the-box. You also need the flexibility to tailor the system without unknowingly creating complexities that will block your upgrade path and drive up future costs with ongoing customization. You want to be very careful about adding third-party solutions to the system; it's best to use only authorized third-party products that allow you to maintain your upgrade path. This may limit your choices but it is critical to the creation of an efficient, upgradeable software platform with easily accessible data.

These best practice strategies enable you to use your system as a management tool, reduce data integration needs (and the related costs), improve member engagement, and drive continuous performance improvement. What association doesn't want that?

What Forward Thinking Leaders are Expecting from Their Technology Investments

We've reviewed traditional system challenges and successful decision-making strategies and now it's time to look at alternatives to help solve your most pressing concerns.

WHAT IF ... there was a better system?

What if this system was a much better management tool because it could enable continuous performance improvement? A system that was built for the way the world works today would be more effective at driving and expanding engagement.

WHAT IF ... a new system could increase revenues while controlling expenses?

What if the system was a much better value because — instead of exploding costs — it actually drove down the on-going expense and complexity of your technology platform? Revenues would go up, costs would go down, and the delta would be a major contribution to your performance. Isn't that what every association needs?

The chart below illustrates the growing revenue and flattening costs over 7 years of a modern engagement management system.

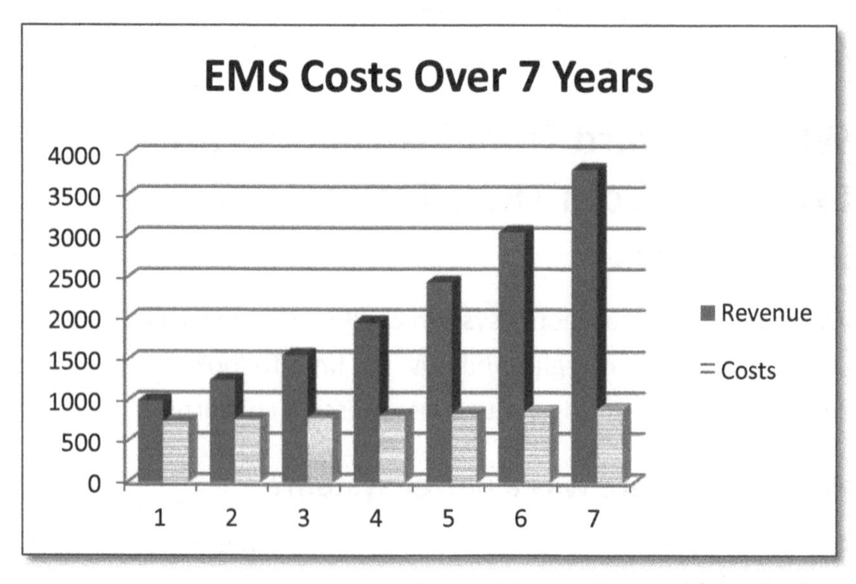

Source: Internal ASI research/client feedback.

WHAT IF ... all of this was in one system?

What if you had a single system that maximized your member engagement and retention, while increasing staff productivity and lowering costs? A traditional AMS system drives up costs due to the duplication of applications required to try to improve member engagement. In the chart below, the applications and services required to support those applications are listed on the right. Based on feedback from clients who previously used AMS systems, we estimate that services accounted for more than 60% of their costs (for integration, customization, difficult upgrades and bug fixes over time.) If you could do all of this in just one system, the majority of the services required would be eliminated and management time would be reduced. The bottom line is that one system would be much less expensive to operate and would yield better results.

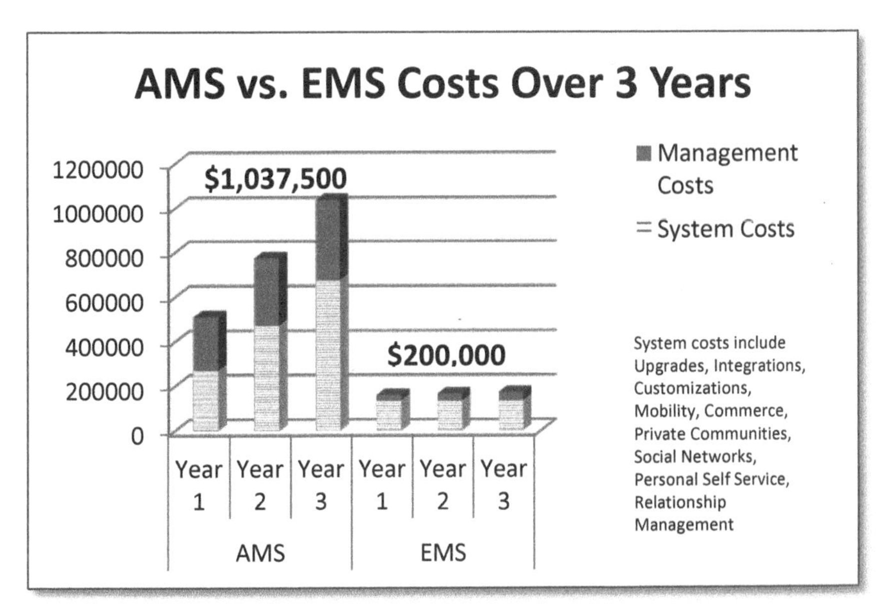

Source: Internal ASI research/client feedback.

WHAT IF ... you could reduce your costs by 80%?

What if a modern engagement management system could be implemented for the actual price quoted in the first year — so all you're paying are small maintenance fees going forward? If you implement an engagement management system in the first year using out-of-the box solutions for the items listed in the chart above, you could reduce your costs by 80%. Even if you tailored the system somewhat, you could still create a dramatic savings over the traditional AMS model.

No need to wonder "What if" any longer; the future is here and it's called an "Engagement Management System" (EMS).

Let us show you how we do this.

iMIS 20 Engagement Management System (EMS)™

With the iMIS 20 Engagement Management System (EMS)™, we are able to offer our clients a major business advantage. The vision for this web-based engagement model is: "Your members can get whatever they need from you via your website and you have a record of it."

iMIS 20 is a full-cycle EMS designed to engage your members and staff anytime, anywhere, and on any device. It's one system, one database that includes:

- Member management
- Self-service
- Social engagement
- Private communities
- Mobile access
- Member websites

And, it's all in a single, seamless cloud-based system.

iMIS 20 greatly reduces data integration needs and complexities while improving member intelligence and driving continuous performance improvement.

Only iMIS 20 provides nearly unlimited flexibility while you stay on the upgrade path (by avoiding expensive custom programming that will raise your long-term costs). The system empowers you to easily create and personalize member self-service, community, and mobile web pages without any programming. By implementing a complete, highly professional engagement management system with thousands of useful features right out of the box, you can extend the functionality of the system without blocking the upgrade path.

Only iMIS 20 eliminates costly integration efforts, gathers better member intelligence for member engagement, and helps you make smarter business decisions. iMIS 20 is built on the RiSE web engagement platform that has the flexibility to work with your existing Content Management System (CMS) or — for many organizations —the power to manage your entire web presence.

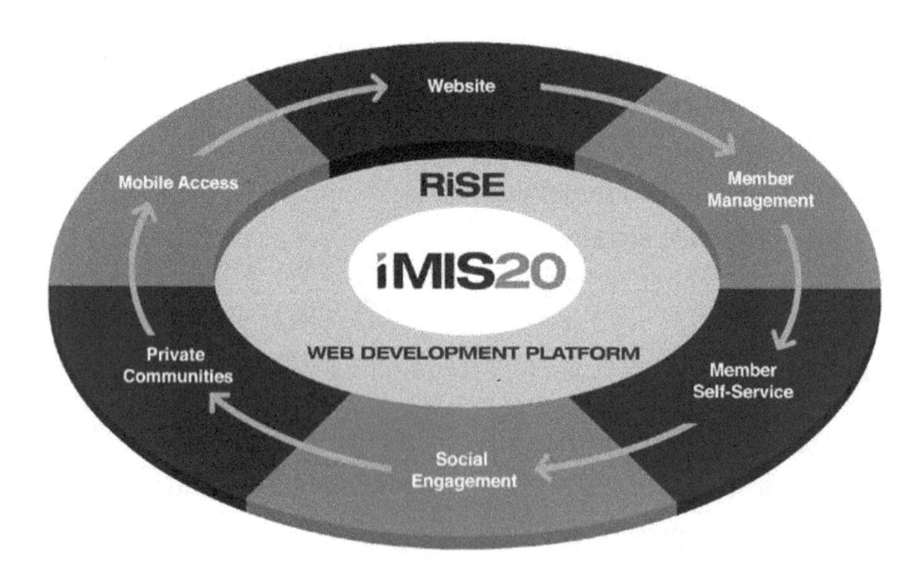

Benefits of an EMS

There are many benefits for an organization to move from the old AMS system approach to an EMS today. The primary reason is that you need to be ready for the future. An Engagement Management System will address most of the modern challenges facing you today; an AMS simply will not. The iMIS 20 EMS was designed for the way your members work today — built on a web engagement platform that will help you make smarter business decisions.

iMIS 20 can help you increase revenues, grow membership and reduce costs. You will also reduce your risk by working with a quality supplier who has been ranked #1 in client satisfaction. More importantly, our approach will help you become a learning organization which will deliver and enable a continuous performance improvement culture that will help you improve your operations consistently year after year after year.

The era of traditional AMS and CRM systems is over because they were never designed to support the way your association works today or how it will operate in the future.

You need the iMIS 20 EMS that will allow your members to register for conferences from their mobile phones after a workout, pay their dues while waiting for a flight, or debate the merits of an important industry initiative in one of your forums. You also need an all-inclusive system that makes your staff more productive and communication easier. With iMIS 20, you'll have one system that engages everyone.

Unique Advantages of Working with Us

iMIS 20 delivers three distinct advantages over alternative systems:

1) By focusing on recruiting, engaging, measuring, and growing, we help your association achieve continuous performance improvement.
2) You can offer your members access to your system for everything they may need — anytime, from wherever they are, from any device. That's our Engagement Management model.
3) RiSE, our powerful web development platform, allows you to fuse your business system and member-oriented websites into one system. This powerful capability allows you to provide members easy, flexible web interfaces to engagement, thereby allowing engagement with your members to sky rocket.

Plus, in addition to all the advantages we've already discussed, ASI's global sales and service network has made iMIS 20 the leading solution. For six years straight, the Global Association Software Study (see Addendum for more information) rated iMIS #1 in the two most important areas:

1) **Client Satisfaction:** We were rated number 1 for client satisfaction, being on-time, being on budget, ease-of-use and for performance after implementation. This demonstrates our ability to continuously deliver what our clients are requesting.

2) **Global Market Share**: iMIS has the greatest share of the worldwide association market space and we have a greater percentage than the next two competitors *combined*.

Chapter 5 – The Results: Achieving Continuous Performance Improvement

At the end of the day, what matters most to your organization's future is that you improve engagement/retention, increase revenue, control your costs, and maximize your overall organizational performance. In other words, you achieve continuous performance improvement.

What is Performance Improvement?

Performance improvement is a measure of the degree to which the output of a particular business process or procedure achieves its goals. Based on results, the processes or procedures can then be modified to increase output, efficiency, or efficacy. Performance improvement as a measure may be applied to either individual or organizational performance.

In associations and membership organizations, performance improvement strategies are changes conceived and implemented by managers and the governing body that are designed to measure current levels of performance and improve them. The primary goal is to increase your organization's effectiveness and efficiency, enhancing your ability to deliver goods or services. A by-product of this activity is the reflective review of goals and objectives. The very act of measuring performance may reveal that your goals and objectives need adjustment. Continuous performance improvement is the bright star for which all associations should reach.

For associations and membership organizations, the objective of continuous performance improvement falls into expected management areas:

- Increasing revenue
- Decreasing expenses
- Mitigating risk

To increase revenue, your association must become an engagement management organization. The measure of success is always how completely members consider your association critical and prove it by their ongoing involvement. On your side, you must always be working towards encouraging members to consider your organization as their primary source of information on the Internet. This facilitates direct and indirect marketing of the value of your association to your constituents, thereby realizing greater participation of members, turning constituents into adherents and, in the best case, enthusiasts.

Decreasing expenses can be realized by freeing the staff to work on more valuable objectives for your association. This can be achieved by moving the management of member data from the staff to the member by way of self-service. Further, the automation of mundane tasks — such as sending emails, reminders, and notifications — can further remove tasks from staff.

You can mitigate risk by making sure that systems are not only secure, but that every effort is being made to assure ongoing success in this and all other areas of organizational endeavor. A system must constantly be tested for potential intrusions, to guard against the unauthorized access of Payment Card Information (PCI) or Personal Identifying Information (PII), such as the intrusions recently experienced by Target®. Achieving PCI compliance using a validated payment application is another way to prevent potential risk. Finally, you and your staff must constantly monitor the results of all efforts to reduce the impact of unsuccessful campaigns.

To achieve performance improvement, associations must ensure that their Business Strategy and Engagement Management Strategy (sometimes referred to as Digital Strategy) are one and the same. Once aligned, the challenge is to determine what to measure, and how. These measures may be in the form of metrics, key performance indicators (KPIs) or Big Data analytics.

The following is an example of a not-for-profit organization's strategy map, which drives its efforts:

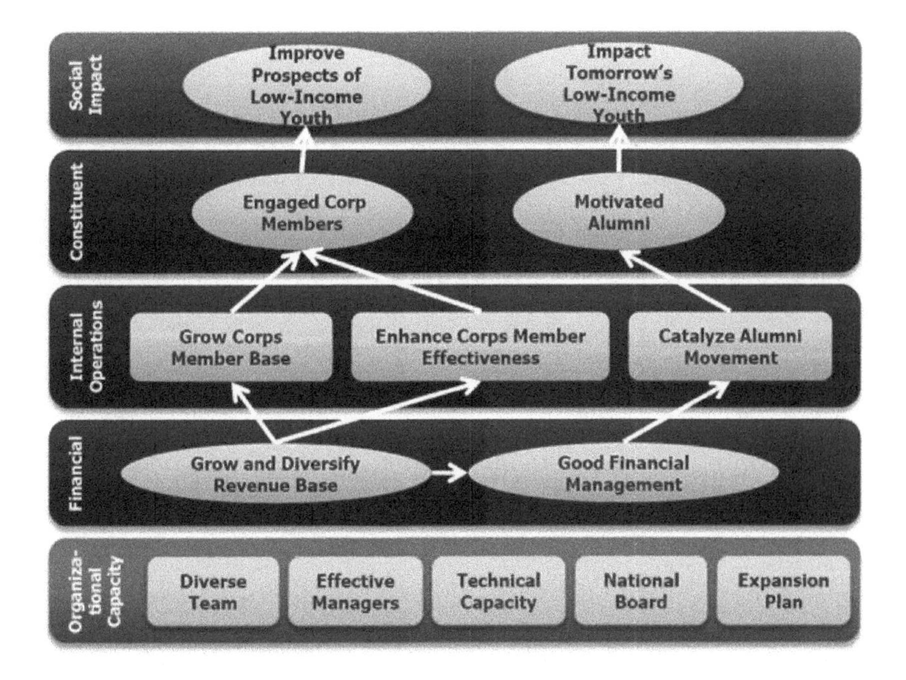

Once measurements have been determined, associations must consciously become learning organizations by interpreting or analyzing the results of these measurables. The results may indicate the success of a particular effort, thereby encouraging you to continue down this path. If results are negative, then you need to determine another approach to achieve better results. Finally, you must put the findings into practice. Without this step, the same mistakes will continue to be made.

The following is a performance improvement cycle that each association should go through to achieve continuous performance improvement:

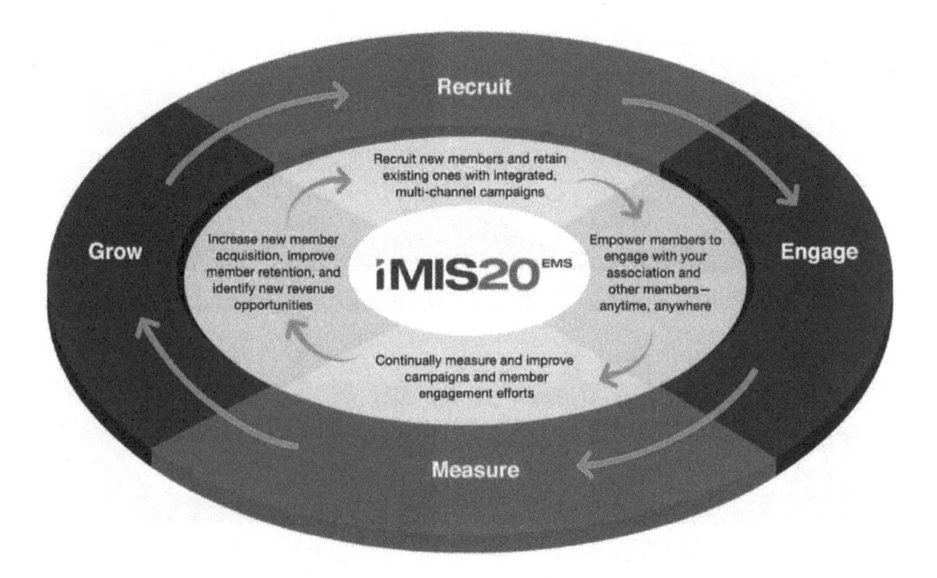

Associations must constantly encourage participation not only by acquiring new members, but also by urging current members to increase their participation. This might be achieved by encouraging them to attend events, purchase products, mentor younger/newer members, or involve themselves in a constant flow of creative activities invented by your organization and designed to enable members to achieve their professional and personal goals.

It's important to recognize that the primary means of communication in the Internet age is social media. Without forgetting that there is certainly value in personal contact, every organization should wield the power of the Internet to deepen the effectiveness of its activities — which, in the end, are communications-related. Because, what is engagement, really? It's ongoing communication that provokes ongoing action, whether that's in the form of conferences, seminars, discussions within communities, donations, or any other examples of involvement. But you cannot determine the success or failure of your strategies without measurement. For each effort, there must be articulated goals and metrics to determine success. When the progress of each effort is measured and then compared to established goals, it will assist in determining your next course of action. This can be accomplished through simple reports or by using a dashboard to visually display the results of these tasks.

Analyzing results enables your organization to grow as successful efforts are repeated and unsuccessful efforts are modified.

One of the best ways to understand the measure of your organization is through a visual analysis of your data using a dashboard. The following is an example of a potential "Events" dashboard:

This sample dashboard reflects important measures for an association's events. The organization can see levels of attainment, relative registrations by member type, and even lists of upcoming events. From this information, staff can quickly determine how each event is performing and determine if other actions are required, such as increased marketing to obtain greater participation.

All learning organizations have unique requirements to measure, but most associations have some standard key performance indicators (KPIs) that measure the organization's direction .

Some of the common KPIs are:

- New member acquisition as a percentage of members
- Renewal rate
- Conversion rate
- Membership strength compared to prior year
- New visitors to association website
- Activities per member
- Financial activities per member
- Committee participation per member
- Emails per member
- Direct mailings per member
- Event registrations per member
- Increase in total membership over prior year
- Number of Continuing Professional Development (CPD) events per month

Once you've determined your specific KPIs, you can then develop a scorecard that reflects results.

Continuous performance improvement is more than just taking measurements. It requires you to align your business strategy with all of your initiatives. Continuous performance improvement then measures those initiatives to determine what new actions to take. A learning organization can turn the results into new actions, which can then improve your overall performance . This is not a one-time effort but a continuous effort, so your association can iteratively improve. Following all these steps enables you to realize continuous performance improvement.

We Can Ensure Continuous Performance Improvement

Best practices may sound easy, but that's only in a perfect world. Our research shows many organizations aren't using the most optimal strategies for member management, which means they fail to reach optimal performance levels.

iMIS 20 can help you to reduce costs, maximize revenue, lower your risk, enhance engagement and improve organizational performance. Let's now take a look at how we've proven this.

To achieve continuous performance improvement, several elements are absolutely vital:

- A clear strategy with long-range resource investment planning approved by the board that's currently being implemented
- Consistent discipline in measuring results and performance that allows management to be proactive and avoid external demands and crisis management

- A nimble management system for configuration and change management to accelerate member engagement
- Departmental processes that encourage growth
- All-in-one member management systems that ease staff burden and increase member convenience
- Top-rated, on-going staff training that increases operational productivity
- A single system with real-time data reporting/analysis for more informed decision making
- Accurate member intelligence that allows for personalization and extends life time value

Our expert staff of Performance Improvement Specialists and consultants will work with you to align your organization with all of the above. iMIS 20 was designed to address all of these elements once a client is positioned correctly to take advantage of them.

We Can Reduce Your Costs

Over a three-year period, the iMIS 20 EMS will cost about five times less than a traditional system. Sound unbelievable? It's true. And, it's because most organizations look at the initial cost of a new system and don't consider the related costs for ongoing customization programming, integration with new technologies, integration between disparate systems, related staff/management costs to maintain the system, and other "hidden costs."

Here's an example: The chart below compares the costs of an iMIS 20 EMS system that can address all of the "system costs"— right out-of-the-box — and what that same solution would cost if using a traditional model. It's a 5X difference — what organization can afford to pay 5 times more than they planned to and be locked into this for 5 to 7 years or more?

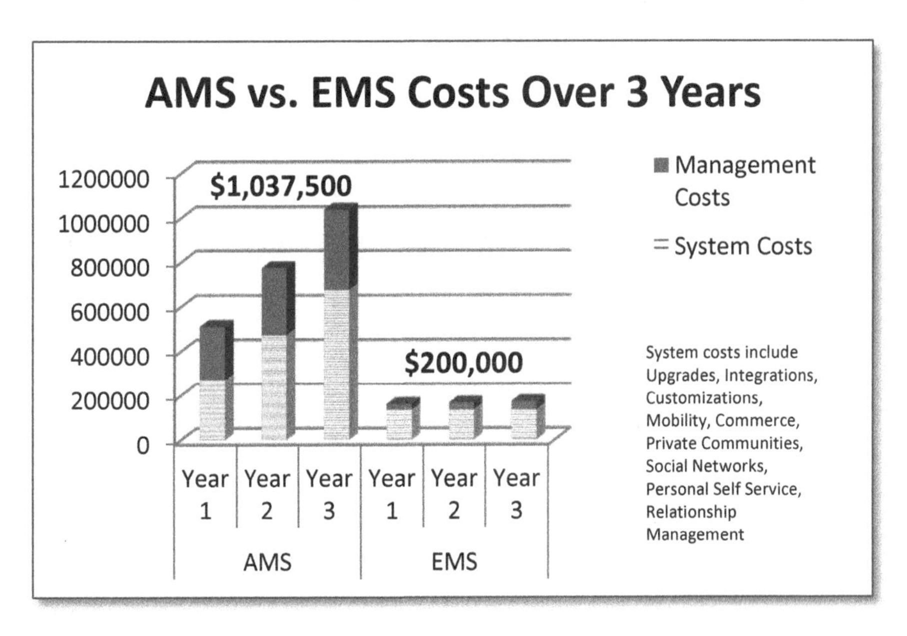

We Can Deliver Strong ROI

It's entirely possible to increase revenue from strong member engagement/retention while at the same time decreasing costs as a result of smart, well-informed decisions. You can do this if you have a modern system like the iMIS 20 EMS, along with the right programs, tools and services from ASI, your trusted advisor!

The graph below shows what you can achieve over a seven-year period with iMIS 20; nearly flat costs and fast-rising revenues.

Notice how the revenue line grows strong while the cost line barely increases. This is how the iMIS 20 EMS delivers a strong return on your system investment that can then be reinvested in your organization.

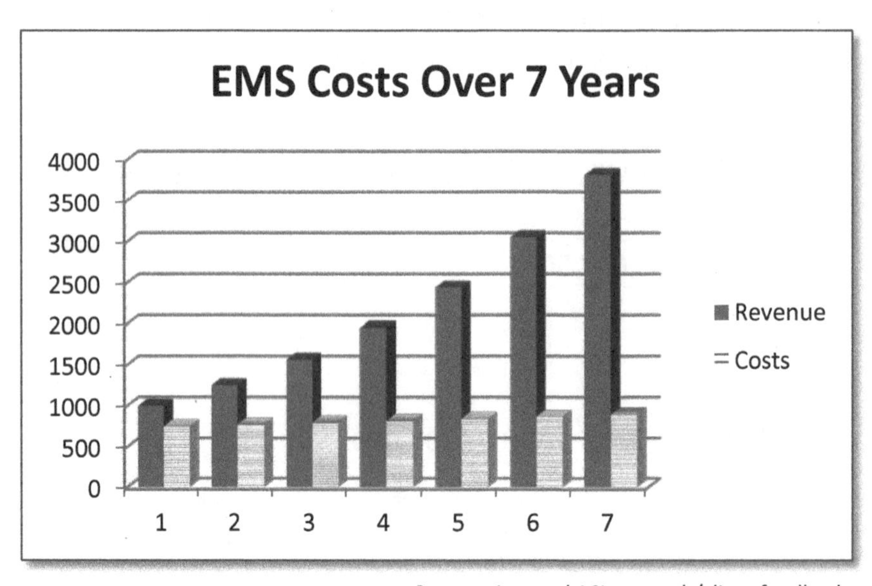

Source: Internal ASI research/client feedback.

We Exceed Expectations: Client Success Stories

At this stage, we'd like to share a few success stories of clients who have followed the best practices we've outlined and have achieved some of the goals we know you want to achieve. To read about more client success please visit www.advsol.com/success.

National Recreation and Park Association

The National Recreation and Park Association (NRPA) is the leading advocacy organization dedicated to the advancement of public parks, recreation and conservation.

Their mission is to advance parks, recreation, and environmental conservation efforts that enhance the quality of life for all people. NRPA has more than 40,000 members, primarily parks and recreation professionals.

> ***"NRPA's ability to more than double its membership in just 16 months -- while still maintaining excellent customer service -- is attributable in part to our use of iMIS. We now have the tools in place to maximize staff efficiency and make sound business decisions about future initiatives."***

The Challenge

The organization determined there was a need to boost its presence in the market and increase membership -- so they created a new agency-based membership package that allowed for greater inclusion of parks and recreation professionals. The upside potential for this initiative was huge and they needed a system that would support a surge in members but also maintain quality customer service.

To accommodate the new members, NRPA knew it needed a website with the latest self-service tools -- and it was vital to the organization that all NRPA-related purchases flow into a central checkout basket. NRPA also needed to be able to easily report on the progress of its initiatives.

The Solution

NRPA used iMIS to create automated processes to generate everything from support emails for membership, certifications and meetings to follow-up letters, coupon codes, reporting, CEU Audits and staff notifications.

NRPA also increased member self-service with web offerings to join/renew, donate, buy products, maintain CEUs, and register for events -- and they could process all NRPA purchases through a single checkout. NRPA was also able to create integrated reports on the status of their goals using key performance indicators such as membership counts, revenue, renewals, market penetration and engagement.

The Results

Within 16 months of starting the new initiative, NRPA membership more than doubled -- from 19,100 members to 40,000. Yet, the organization only added one new customer service position to keep up with the increased demand. With iMIS, NRPA has streamlined its processes and freed up customer service staff to focus on the organization's mission and work directly with members rather than on manual tasks.

Members enjoy a convenient, seamless experience and staff is able to quickly mine data to make more informed decisions. With the core systems in place, NRPA is confident about its ability to continue to grow and support its membership going forward.

The International Underwriting Association of London

The International Underwriting Association of London (IUA) is the focal representative and market organization for non-Lloyd's international and wholesale insurance and reinsurance companies operating in the London Market. It exists to promote and enhance the business environment for international insurance and reinsurance companies operating in or through London.

The Challenge

IUA needed to replace their website to enhance member resources and improve resource allocation internally. The goal was to develop a resource that would enhance and expand communication with members, improve member access to IUA information and documents, and encourage greater engagement in the association.

The Solution

IUA opted for a new database, using the iMIS system to better manage several aspects of the organization's day-to-day work. One of the key developments was the creation of IUA Communities -- online interest groups with content specifically tailored to a particular class of business or business specialty. This enabled market professionals to find information directly relevant to their own work.

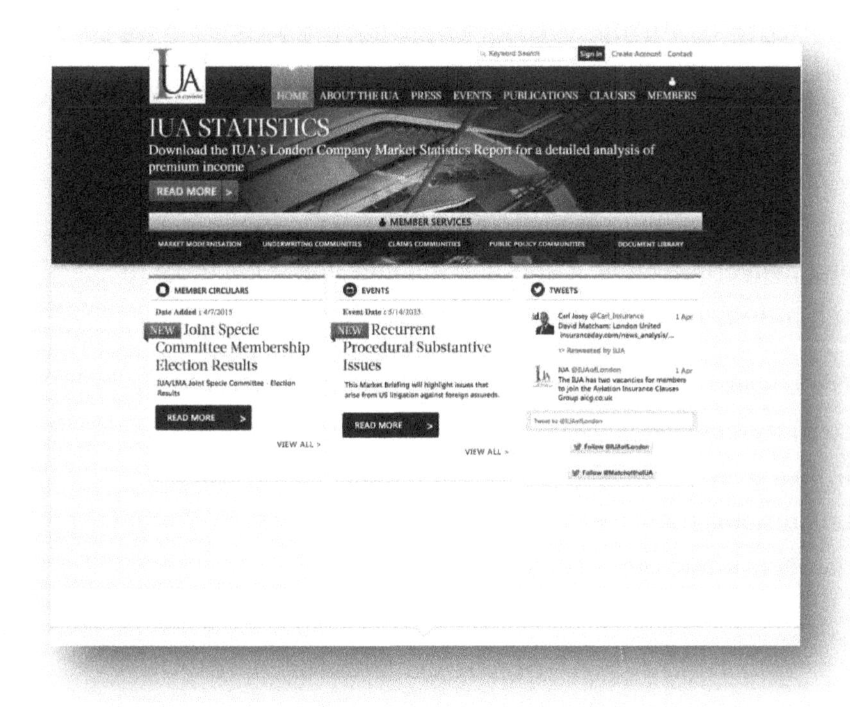

The Results

The new website offers additional information on all aspects of the association's work and creates virtual communities around important market issues. It is much easier for members to stay abreast of the latest news, market developments and the projects undertaken by individual IUA committees. The site provides community pages that cover a wide range of topics, advanced keyword search capabilities, a publications library, useful industry links, and relevant IUA reference documents -- all to create a better business environment for insurance and reinsurance companies.

Institute of Public Works Engineering Australasia

The Institute of Public Works Engineering Australasia (IPWEA) is a professional organization providing member services and advocacy for those involved in and delivering public works and engineering services to the community in both Australia and New Zealand.

The organization is a federated body comprising an Australasia central body and seven divisions with more than 3,300 members from a wide range of professions, including engineers, technicians, public works directors, contractors, consultants, managers, and other technical staff.

> ***"Our plan wasn't about just having a new database or a new website. It was a strategy that aimed to completely rebuild and fully integrate our business systems. iMIS is the backbone of all our work."***

The Challenge

Each division of the IPWEA had its own member database that was updated manually. Contact information wasn't consistent across the databases, duplication was common, communication with members across divisions was difficult, and there was no single location to confirm IPWEA membership in real time.

The organization wanted to integrate its financial, marketing and business systems and improve communications with its members/contacts. As part of the rebuild of its business systems, the IPWEA needed to consolidate the siloed databases, improve its online presence, and develop a professional networking platform.

The Solution

With iMIS the IPWEA was able to integrate its website, databases, email marketing, orders, event registration, microsites, discussion forums, and online communities. Some offerings were provided as an opt-in service to divisions. IPWEA was able to completely rebuild and integrate its systems and iMIS was central to its efforts.

The overall system has helped the IPWEA provide more consistent messaging/communications to members as well as provide real-time database integration to a new interactive website with user-generated content management facilities, networking opportunities, and more.

The Results

IPWEA Australasia runs all transactions and invoicing through iMIS, including membership fees of most divisions, event and workshop registrations, and back-office subscription and bookstore purchases.

This centralized system ensures that data is consistently up-to-date. The new business systems are helping the IPWEA add capacity within the organization enabling it to offer opt-in business services to all divisions.

The IPWEA believes iMIS is built to accommodate its future. Membership structures and the integrated systems in place allow IPWEA to continually increase and improve engagement with members and the broader public works industry.

Girl Guides of Canada - Guides du Canada

Girl Guides of Canada-Guides du Canada has been the country's leading organization dedicated solely to girls for more than 100 years.

With 90,000 members, this organization continually provides opportunities for girls of all walks of life to discover, explore, be adventurous and make a difference -- while building life skills that increase confidence and self-esteem.

The Challenge

Girl Guides recognized that it needed a new system that could help improve efficiency, reduce substantial paperwork burdens on staff, and make the joining process simpler. Girl Guides needed a system that was compatible with industry standard technology, could grow with the organization, and would be easy for its stakeholders to use. Most importantly, they wanted to implement the latest tools that would help them provide outstanding service to members.

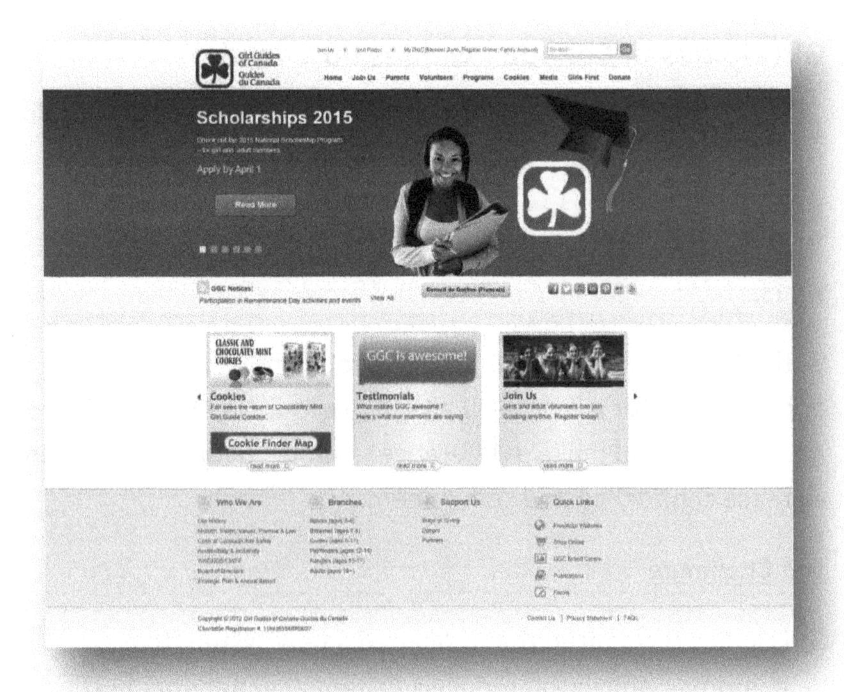

The Solution

Girl Guides chose iMIS because it was able to address all of its challenges at the time and had the flexibility and scalability to adapt as needs change in the future.

With the iMIS system, Girl Guides could streamline operations, improve processes, reduce administrative burdens, track trends, report on results, and provide more timely and personalized service to their members. The system also ensured that the organization continued to stay true to its governance requirements.

The Results

Stakeholders are extremely pleased with the scope of information at their fingertips, the functionality of the system, and its reliability. The Girl Guides' fun, interactive website is powered by iMIS and allows the organization to provide more personalized content, self-service functionality, and a simpler way of joining. It contributes to the overall member experience and the organization's extremely high retention rates.

By removing manual processes, staff and volunteers can focus on the organization's core objectives -- and membership continues to grow as a result.

Chapter 6 — Next Steps: Success Partnership Program (SPP)

The Success Partnership Program (SPP) is designed to assist senior-level executives of larger associations and membership organizations get the most out of their technology investments. We help you plan and execute the alignment of your operations with strategy. Our objective is to partner with you as your trusted advisor to permanently enable continuous performance improvement within your organization.

Visit www.advsol.com/sppvideo to see a message from Robert Alves about the value of the SPP.

The first step is our 25-point complementary, no-risk Success Assessment™ (see Chapter 2 — Assessing Your Current Situation). We compare your operations to industry best practices and prepare a report that is yours to keep. And based on our findings we determine whether your organization is a good fit for this program.

If you continue with the program, we next conduct a hands-on workshop to review the assessment with you and key staff. Many clients move from there to a smooth and efficient *"Performance Improvement Preview"* to help them see the potential of working with us toward continuous performance improvement.

The SPP is designed to help you proactively identify your critical needs quickly, prepare a technology investment plan you can communicate to your Board with confidence that it will align with your organizational strategy, and – if you desire – ensure that anyone you work with in the future can accurately address your issues. This approach ultimately saves you time, money, and significantly reduces your risk of investing in the wrong technology assets and repeating the mistakes you may have made in the past.

To learn more about how the Success Partnership Program (SPP) works see the Addendum.

About the Authors

Robert Alves
Chairman and CEO
Advanced Solutions
International (ASI)

Bob Alves is not your average corporate leader. He is unlike the many CEOs who remain faceless atop an organization chart, far removed from the company's everyday operations. An ASI Founding Partner more than 20 years ago, Bob is involved to this day in every critical aspect of the company – its present and the planning and design of its future.

After receiving his Bachelor of Business Administration degree from George Washington University, Bob went to work in the non-profit industry. He began as founder and President of DISC in 1982, a non-profit technology consulting company. DISC was acquired by software developer Smith Abbott in 1987, where Bob served as Vice President of Corporate Development.

Bob has always had a strong entrepreneurial spirit. After wrestling with the general lack of proper client service and absence of uniform products for the non-profit technology marketplace, he was inspired to found ASI in 1991. Driven by the mission of "keeping clients for life," ASI developed iMIS – advanced, easily upgradeable, and backed by a world-class, global network of trained client support staff.

Don Robertson
President and CTO
Advanced Solutions
International (ASI)

Don Robertson is a widely known architect for positive change in the non-profit software industry, deftly building the future, not with concrete or steel, but with the dynamic processes of software. Don's vision has impacted more than 4,000 non-profits around the world.

Before helping to found ASI in 1991, Don honed his craft with Texas Instruments, American Standard and non-profit software developer Smith Abbott. While providing software consulting services at Smith Abbott, Don was struck by the lack of reliable, flexible and scalable software solutions for not-for-profit organizations.

Determined to remedy the situation, Don dedicated himself to the idea of pioneering software that could effectively manage an organization's constituency, communications and resources. iMIS became that solution. Today, it remains the flagship product of the award winning company he helped create.

As President and Chief Technology Officer (CTO) of ASI, Don works hard every day to advance the company's philosophy through its technology. Don has a deep affection for the non-profit industry, is an ardent supporter of the community and an active participant within it.

About ASI

Advanced Solutions International (ASI) is a recognized global, industry thought leader that focuses on helping associations and not-for-profits increase operational and financial performance through the use of best practices, proven solutions, and ongoing client advisement.

We are the provider of iMIS 20, an Engagement Management System (EMS)™ that enables organizations to engage members, donors, and other constituents anytime, anywhere, from any device.

We also have a global network of nearly 100 partners to provide you with a full range of services to implement and support your iMIS system.

Locations

USA
901 N. Pitt St., Suite 200
Alexandria, VA 22314
1-800-727-8682

Canada
251 Consumers Rd., Suite 1404
Toronto, ON Canada M2J 4R3
1-800-727-8682

Europe
2 Station Court, Imperial Wharf
London SW6 2PY
+44(0)20 3267 0067

Asia-Pacific
Level 22, 459 Collins Street
Melbourne VIC 3000
+61 3 9869 7500

Connect with Us

 www.advsol.com  @advsol  advanced-solutions-international-inc.

Addendum

The Success Partnership Program (SPP)

Overview

ASI's Success Partnership Program (SPP) is a no-risk way to assess, document, and test your specific needs in a real-world environment —using your own data and processes — and to learn exactly how the iMIS 20 Engagement Management System (EMS)™ can help before you decide to invest.

It's more than just a test drive: we work in partnership with you to understand your goals/objectives and then help you find the best methods to continuous performance improvement.

For a nominal engagement fee (which can be applied to your new iMIS system), you'll come away with a highly personalized report that documents everything you need from your next system in order to improve your overall results. You can then use this report to make an informed decision about iMIS — or any other potential system.

Benefits

No Risk

The SPP allows you to validate what you need from a new system before investing.

If you decide iMIS is not for you, you walk away with a finely tuned review report that is a far better predictor of your success than an RFP. No risk, no hassle, no downside.

More Effective

A system chosen through an RFP process rarely meets expectations because the process typically documents and then replicates current inefficiencies. We partner with you to understand your vital business processes, identify any possible gaps, and recommend the best and most modern methods to improve your overall results. We ask the tough questions and help you find the right answers by testing in a real-time, real-world environment.

Faster

In less than 90 days you can complete the program and know precisely what your organization requires and how iMIS can meet those challenges. No long, expensive, frustrating RFP process — and no guesswork.

Lower Cost

RFPs often require extensive staff time to brief multiple vendors over and over and lead to increased staff burden and expenses. The SPP minimizes internal costs, maximizes productivity, and gives a better return on your investment.

2016 Global Membership Performance Report

Executive Summary

ASI is proud to present our second annual Global Benchmark Report on Membership Performance, which explores the results, challenges, and goals of associations across North America, Europe/Middle East/India/Africa (EMEIA), and Asia-Pacific. The survey was conducted in the third quarter of 2015 and includes responses from 734 association and membership organization executives. In conducting our analysis of the data, we observed certain key trends/characteristics of some of the most successful organizations in terms of retention and growth; where relevant, we include these findings as well.

Overall Findings

In ASI's 2015 membership performance survey, it was clear that associations understood the power of member engagement. In 2016, engagement remains the top goal and there are signs that this focus — as well as increasing mobile/online options, replacing outdated member management systems, and updating the website — is having a real impact on one of the most critical metrics for today's associations: retention.

More than three-quarters of all respondents have a 76% or greater overall retention rate, which is a significant increase from 2015. 55% saw a rise in their membership base (up from 48% last year) and 41% have seen increases in engagement.

While many organizations are taking the necessary actions to achieve their goals and overcome stated challenges, not everyone has gotten the memo. A lack of adequate reporting tools and an inability to measure member engagement continue to plague too many associations and membership organizations.

The overall tone of this year's survey was very hopeful: more than half of all participants reported they are very optimistic about their future over the next 5 years.

Top Goals & Challenges

In addition to engagement and retention, executives are also concerned with acquiring new members. With the rising cost of new acquisitions, these organizations may wish to focus their attention on keeping the existing member base satisfied. To boost engagement and address measurement shortfalls, associations need a centralized member management system that aligns operations with their core business strategy and puts them on a path to long-term, continuous performance improvement.

Engagement/Retention

While retention is a top goal for membership organizations, the fact that 65% have seen declining or stagnant retention rates in the past year seems to indicate that they have not yet found the optimal methods to support that objective.

Engagement is vital to retaining members, but less than one-third (31%) of respondents currently have a formal plan to measure it. A centralized member management system that integrates data with the website could provide vital intelligence.

Reporting

Too many executives checked the "Don't Know" box when it came to specific questions about engagement, retention, and online transactions. While a lack of adequate reporting capabilities was a top challenge in both 2015 and 2016, the latest survey shows no real improvement in this area.

To enhance reporting, association and membership organization executives should explore the latest member management systems on the market. New options are available that allow organizations to test systems in a real-world environment with their own data and processes to determine their specific needs before deciding to invest.

Web/Mobile/Social

65% of the most successful organizations (those with 90+% retention) redesigned their website within the past 2 years and 43% used Responsive Web Design (RWD) — an exceptional cost- and time-saver.

There's been a definite increase in mobile/ online transactions over the past year. Of those associations and membership organizations that processed more than one-half of their new joins and renewals online, 67% grew their base and 48% increased overall engagement.

While Facebook, Twitter, and LinkedIn are used pretty extensively, social media is not regarded as a highly effective channel for new member joins or renewals.

Technology

The most successful associations and membership organizations ensure their business strategy drives their technology investments — they continuously learn about themselves from their operational activities. One of the best ways to do this is with a centralized management system that integrates member data with the website. The 2016 survey shows that many associations already "get" this. 55% of the most successful organizations (those with 90+% retention) revealed they have upgraded their member management system within the past two years.

2015 Association Software Global Study

Summary

This is a Lehman Reports™ study conducted by Lehman Associates, an independent research firm. Lehman Associates surveys associations in the USA, Canada, United Kingdom, Australia, and New Zealand with $1m+ in budget. ASI is one of multiple software vendors who subscribe to the study to receive the results.

Implementation Experience

With ASI/iMIS, compared to other vendors, you have a much greater probability of your implementation being on time, the ease of implementation being as expected, and the performance after being implemented as being as expected or better.

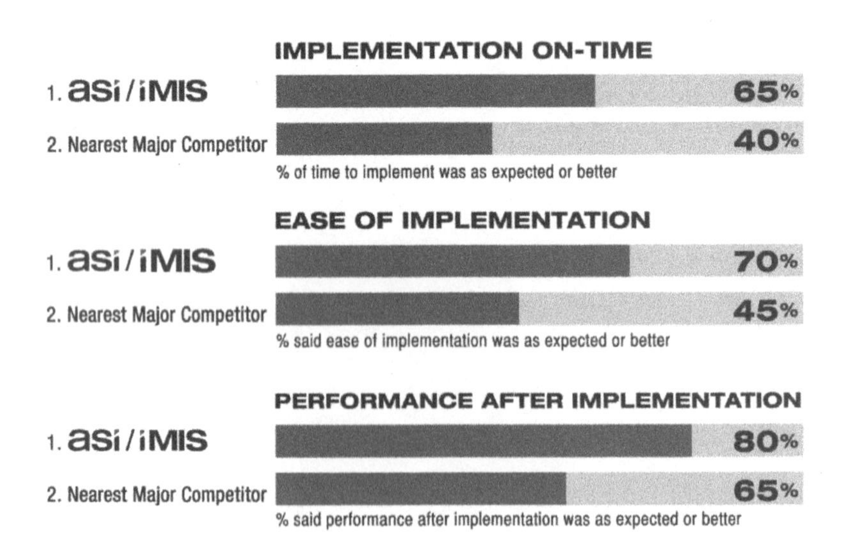

Market Share

ASI/iMIS is the market leader in the USA, Canada, United Kingdom, Australia, and New Zealand by almost three times the nearest competitor.

GLOBAL MARKET SHARE

1. asi / iMIS	31%
2. Nearest Vendor	12%
3. Vendor	6%
4. Vendor	5%
5. Vendor	3%
6. Vendor	2%
7. Vendor	1.5%
8. Vendor	1%
9. Vendor	1%
10. Vendor	1%

% of Installed Base of Products

USA, Canada, Australia/New Zealand, UK

About Lehman Associates

Lehman Associates, LLC, was founded in 1992 to help companies, associations and other non-profits become more successful with better information and insight about markets and constituents, well-constructed strategy to help guide planning and resource allocation, and effective use of online technologies to reach and engage target audiences. The Lehman Reports™ series of industry studies detail the use of technology by associations and other non-profits. For more information, visit www.LehmanConsulting.com and www.LehmanReports.com.